Would You Rather: Gross, Silly, and Totally Bonkers!

500+ Hilarious, Wild & Wacky Questions for Kids, A Giggle-Filled Game and Activity Book for Ages 6-12, Perfect for Boys, Girls, Family Fun, and Game Night

By T J Harvey

Contents

How to Use This Book

This isn't just a book – it's your portable laugh machine, boredom buster, and family bonding tool all rolled into one!

You can play anywhere: in the car, plane or train, at the dinner table, during sleepovers, birthday parties, on rainy days, as icebreakers in the classroom... even in the world's longest queue.

Ways to Play:

- **Classic Play** - Take turns reading and answering.

- **Why, Why, Why?** – Explain why you chose your answer.

- **Team Debate** - Convince others your choice is the best.

- **Lightning Round** - Answer as fast as you can, no thinking!

- **Twist It!** - Change one part of the question to make it sillier.

- **Mystery Pick** - One player reads the question, but everyone has to guess which option they will choose before they reveal it.

- **Reverse Round** - You have to pick the option you'd normally never choose!

Pro Tips for Maximum Fun

- **Mix & Match:** Combine questions from different chapters for extra weirdness.

- **Character Voices:** Answer in a silly accent or as a wacky character.

- **Act It Out:** Pretend your answer is really happening - no holding back!

- **Double Trouble:** Play with two questions at the same time for total chaos.

Extra Challenges:

- **Laugh Trap:** Try to answer without laughing - giggle and you're out!

- **Speed Round:** Set a timer for 5 seconds per answer - fastest wins!

- **Flip the Script:** Swap answers with someone else and defend their choice.

- **True or False:** Before revealing your answer, say "True" or "False." Everyone else guesses whether you're telling the truth about your choice.

Bonkers Leaderboard:

Rate your friends and family after a round of Would You Rather?

Put a ✔ next to the name of the person who wins each round:

- Funniest answer:

- Grossest answer:

- Most creative response:

- Most convincing argument:

- Silliest performance:

- Bravest choice:

Now... turn the page, and let the laughter begin!

Gross-Outs Galore

Prepare for safe but seriously silly "ewww!" moments - perfect for anyone who loves a good giggle with their grossness.

1. Would you rather eat a popsicle made of snot or drink a smoothie made of old socks?

2. Would you rather never stop sneezing boogers or hiccup soap bubbles every time you blink?

3. Would you rather eat a worm sandwich or drink a cup of pickle juice mixed with ketchup?

4. Would you rather wake up covered in slime covered marshmallows or in bubble-goo noodles that sing?

5. Would you rather smell like a fart forever or have stinky feet so strong they knock people over?

6. Would you rather have spaghetti made of rainbows for hair or sneeze out jelly beans?

7. Would you rather pick your nose in front of your crush or step in a mystery slime barefoot?

8. Would you rather wear underwear on your head forever or have toilet paper stuck to your foot forever?

9. Would you rather always smell like rotten eggs, or have burps that sound like a trombone?

10. Would you rather burp every time you talk or have hiccups every time you laugh?

11. Would you rather eat booger-flavoured jelly beans or earwax-flavoured ice cream?

12. Would you rather clean a giant's armpits or brush a dragon's teeth?

13. Would you rather sit on a whoopee cushion in class every day or hiccup like a goose in an elevator full of people?

14. Would you rather have drool that never stops or sweat that smells like tuna fish?

15. Would you rather wear clothes made of cheese or shoes made of wet bread?

16. Would you rather eat cereal with ketchup or pizza with chocolate syrup?

17. Would you rather take a bubble bath in slime or brush your teeth with mustard?

18. Would you rather pick up dog poop with your bare hands or take a mud bath with worms?

19. Would you rather get burped on by a giant or sneezed on by a troll?

20. Would you rather sleep in a bed full of mashed potatoes or a bathtub full of gravy?

Food Fiascos

From weird flavour mash-ups to wacky table manners - this menu is guaranteed to make you laugh, not lick your lips!

21. Would you rather eat spaghetti with chocolate sauce or ice cream with ketchup?

22. Would you rather have popcorn for hair or cotton candy for eyebrows?

23. Would you rather drink a milkshake made of pickles or eat a doughnut filled with mustard?

24. Would you rather burp whipped cream or sneeze sprinkles?

25. Would you rather eat soup with chopsticks or mashed potatoes with a straw?

26. Would you rather have broccoli-flavoured ice cream or pizza-flavoured toothpaste?

27. Would you rather wear pants made of fruit roll-ups or a shirt made of waffles?

28. Would you rather eat cookies that scream or a taco that tells jokes?

29. Would you rather have pancakes for hands or cupcakes for feet?

30. Would you rather never eat sweet things again or only eat weird combinations forever?

31. Would you rather eat a salad made of candy or a burger made of cake?

32. Would you rather drink soda that fizzes out your nose or juice that glows in the dark?

33. Would you rather only eat bright green food or food that moves on your plate?

34. Would you rather eat spaghetti that wiggles or a sandwich that growls?

35. Would you rather your snacks talk back or your dinner runs away from you?

36. Would you rather eat a hot dog with jelly beans or tacos filled with cereal?

37. Would you rather wear a peanut butter helmet or jelly shoes?

38. Would you rather eat ice cream with hot sauce or doughnuts with garlic frosting?

39. Would you rather have a never-ending pie fight or a ketchup hose that won't turn off?

40. Would you rather have a fridge that sings or a microwave that giggles when it's done?

Animal Antics

Wild, wacky, and wonderfully ridiculous - get ready for critter chaos like you've never imagined.

41. Would you rather ride a giant hamster to school or fly on a giant duck?

42. Would you rather have a tail that wags when you're excited or ears that flap when you're nervous?

43. Would you rather talk to animals only in rhymes or roar like a lion whenever you're happy?

44. Would you rather smell like a skunk or have a goat that follows you everywhere?

45. Would you rather be tickled by a thousand kittens or hugged by a gorilla wearing a tutu?

46. Would you rather hop like a kangaroo or waddle like a penguin forever?

47. Would you rather have feathers instead of hair or webbed feet?

48. Would you rather have a penguin splash water on you once a day or a hamster hide your snacks

49. Would you rather bark every time you laugh or moo every time you talk?

50. Would you rather wear a chicken on your head or carry a pig in your backpack?

51. Would you rather have a pet that talks back or sings opera?

52. Would you rather wrestle a jellyfish or tickle a tarantula?

53. Would you rather eat ants for breakfast or worms for dinner?

54. Would you rather be chased by a group of giggling hyenas or a dancing bear?

55. Would you rather be stuck in a car with a skunk or on a boat with a dolphin that never stops singing?

56. Would you rather have a raccoon as a roommate or a parrot that tattles on you?

57. Would you rather be best friends with a wobbly giraffe or a coughing crocodile?

58. Would you rather ride a turtle across the country or an ostrich to the moon?

59. Would you rather have squirrel teeth or frog legs?

60. Would you rather be part-human, part-octopus or part-human, part-chicken?

Silly Superpowers

Super speed? Laser eyes? Or just the power to burp glitter? The choice is yours - hero or hilarious!

61. Would you rather have super speed but only while doing the chicken dance or fly but only two feet off the ground?

62. Would you rather shoot alphabet spaghetti from your fingers or sneeze confetti tornadoes?

63. Would you rather be invisible, but only when you sing opera or teleport, and always end up in a pie?

64. Would you rather have x-ray vision that only works on potatoes or the power to talk to ants?

65. Would you rather bounce like a rubber ball or stretch like a wad of gum?

66. Would you rather grow ten feet tall every time you're embarrassed or shrink whenever you laugh?

67. Would you rather turn into a banana when scared or a balloon when surprised?

68. Would you rather glow like a flashlight when excited or make foghorn noises when angry?

69. Would you rather have sneezes so strong they blow papers away or laughs so loud they shake buildings?

70. Would you rather control jelly with your mind or be able to summon socks at will?

71. Would you rather have super strength but only in your pinky toe or super hearing but only during thunderstorms?

72. Would you rather fly but only backwards or have laser eyes that only work on cupcakes?

73. Would you rather teleport into toilets by mistake or turn invisible only when no one is looking?

74. Would you rather turn everything you touch into pudding or have your hair grow five inches every minute?

75. Would you rather have a cape that farts or boots that sing show tunes?

76. Would you rather shoot mashed potatoes from your nose or ketchup from your ears?

77. Would you rather have a tongue that glows or a belly button that honks?

78. Would you rather be magnetic to spoons or stick to every chair you sit on?

79. Would you rather hiccup bubbles or sneeze confetti every day?

80. Would you rather have super stinky feet or a voice that sounds like a kazoo?

81. Would you rather be able to fly, but only while sneezing, or turn invisible, but only when no one is looking?

82. Would you rather have super strength, but only in your pinky toe, or super speed, but only when hopping?

83. Would you rather shoot sausages from your fingers or sneeze soap foam?

84. Would you rather have a belly button that plays music or eyebrows that wiggle when danger is near?

85. Would you rather be able to burp your ABCs perfectly or hiccup rainbows?

86. Would you rather turn into a popsicle when you get cold or melt like cheese when you're embarrassed?

87. Would you rather be able to jump over buildings but land in jelly or talk to animals but they only gossip?

88. Would you rather glow in the dark or have a nose that beeps like a car horn?

89. Would you rather teleport but only into swimming pools or be invisible but only when you're singing?

90. Would you rather stretch like a rubber band or bounce like a beach ball?

91. Would you rather talk to plants or understand what bugs say?

92. Would you rather be able to change colours like a chameleon or puff up like a balloon when surprised?

93. Would you rather have laser eyes that toast marshmallows or super hearing that only works with whispers?

94. Would you rather have a cape that makes you float or boots that make you dance?

95. Would you rather turn into a giant cupcake or shrink into a jelly bean?

96. Would you rather have a voice that echoes like a cave or one that sounds like a duck?

97. Would you rather have rubber-hose arms or hotdog legs?

98. Would you rather sneeze exploding mini muffins or burp bubbles?

99. Would you rather be super fast but only while crawling or super strong but only while whispering?

100. Would you rather wear a superhero costume every day or talk in a superhero narrator's voice forever?

101. Would you rather have eyebrows that shoot lasers or toes that glow in the dark?

102. Would you rather always float one inch off the ground or bounce as if you're on a trampoline?

103. Would you rather be able to roar like a dinosaur or chirp like a cricket when you're excited?

104. Would you rather have hair that grows really fast or fingernails that glow different colours?

105. Would you rather be able to turn invisible but only when holding your breath or fly but only in circles?

106. Would you rather have jelly for bones or marshmallows for muscles?

107. Would you rather be able to stick to walls like a gecko or puff up like a pufferfish when scared?

108. Would you rather sneeze out popcorn or snore like a lion?

109. Would you rather have arms that stretch like spaghetti or legs that spin like wheels?

110. Would you rather have a voice that sounds like a robot or only be able to talk in riddles?

111. Would you rather be able to smell emotions or hear colours?

112. Would you rather have a moustache made of feathers or eyelashes made of spaghetti?

113. Would you rather have hiccups that make you teleport or yawns that make you fly?

114. Would you rather be made of bubblegum or be invisible but smell like cheese?

115. Would you rather change into a different animal every time you sneeze or hiccup bubbles every time you laugh?

116. Would you rather shoot whipped cream from your ears or ketchup from your belly button?

117. Would you rather blink and make things float or snap and make silly noises happen?

118. Would you rather be able to spin super fast like a tornado or bounce like a rubber ball?

119. Would you rather have a tail that wags when you're happy or ears that flap when you're nervous?

120. Would you rather glow like a lightbulb when you're embarrassed or squeak like a toy when you're surprised?

Toilet Time Trouble

Flush away boredom with these bathroom brain-busters - just don't laugh so hard you fall off the seat!

121. Would you rather accidentally flush your socks or your homework?

122. Would you rather have a sink that sings or a mirror that tells jokes?

123. Would you rather sit on a freezing toilet seat or one that's super sticky?

124. Would you rather clog the toilet at school or at your grandma's house?

125. Would you rather have a toilet paper roll that screams when used or one that's alive and tries to run away?

126. Would you rather slip on a banana peel in the bathroom or fall into a giant tub of toothpaste?

127. Would you rather have to plunge a toilet full of chocolate syrup or one full of porridge?

128. Would you rather make a squeaky-toy noise every time you flush or hiccup when someone else does?

129. Would you rather drop your phone in the toilet or your lunch?

130. Would you rather use leaves as toilet paper or yesterday's newspaper pages?

131. Would you rather the bathroom smell like burnt popcorn forever or rotting fish?

132. Would you rather brush your teeth with hot sauce or with pickle juice?

133. Would you rather take bubble baths in pudding full of rubber ducks or showers in milkshake with mini chocolate bears?

134. Would you rather be trapped in a porta-potty during a thunderstorm or a public restroom during a power outage?

135. Would you rather find a spider in your toilet or a frog in your sink?

136. Would you rather have your toilet talk back or your toothbrush sing opera?

137. Would you rather always clog the toilet or run out of toilet paper?

138. Would you rather poop glitter or pee lemonade?

139. Would you rather flush a toilet that roars or sings pop songs?

140. Would you rather have a bathroom made of cheese or marshmallows?

Wacky What-Ifs

Totally bonkers scenarios that will twist your brain into a pretzel - in the best way possible.

141. Would you rather have jelly beans for teeth or waffles for ears?

142. Would you rather bounce everywhere like a kangaroo or slide around like you're on ice?

143. Would you rather only be able to whisper or only be able to yell?

144. Would you rather always wear clothes backwards or shoes on the wrong feet?

145. Would you rather have stretchy cheese fingers or broccoli toes?

146. Would you rather have a nose that honks or ears that wiggle when you lie?

147. Would you rather cry maple syrup or sweat soda?

148. Would you rather always walk in slow motion or skip instead of walking?

149. Would you rather have rainbow-coloured teeth or glow-in-the-dark fingernails?

150. Would you rather always smell like onions or always sound like a duck?

151. Would you rather talk like a robot or like a pirate?

152. Would you rather turn into a chair when you sit or a lamp when you stand still?

153. Would you rather your elbows be on your knees or your nose on your belly button?

154. Would you rather get stuck inside a video game or a board game?

155. Would you rather live inside a bouncy castle or on a trampoline roof?

156. Would you rather hiccup bubbles or burp butterflies?

157. Would you rather wear socks on your hands forever or mittens on your feet?

158. Would you rather have a refrigerator for a head or a couch for a body?

159. Would you rather your hair be made of string cheese or worms?

160. Would you rather laugh like a donkey or snort like a pig when you giggle?

161. Would you rather live in a house made of pizza or sleep in a bed made of marshmallows?

162. Would you rather turn invisible when you hiccup or fly for five seconds every time you sneeze?

163. Would you rather hop everywhere like a bunny or waddle like a penguin?

164. Would you rather your voice change to a cartoon character's once a day or only speak in rhymes?

165. Would you rather live in a world made of LEGOs or one made of whipped cream?

166. Would you rather wear roller skates forever or never be able to take off a superhero cape?

167. Would you rather eat everything with chopsticks, even soup, or drink everything through a giant twisty straw?

168. Would you rather your hair grow an inch every hour or your fingernails glow in the dark?

169. Would you rather have a talking backpack or a pet pencil that gives silly advice?

170. Would you rather be able to shrink to the size of a jellybean or grow as tall as a giraffe whenever you want?

171. Would you rather live in a treehouse with monkeys or a pillow fort with talking teddy bears?

172. Would you rather slide to school on a giant banana peel or arrive riding a pogo stick buffalo?

173. Would you rather have to sing everything you say or dance every time you hear a bell?

174. Would you rather trade places with your pet for a day or become your favourite toy?

175. Would you rather time travel using a toilet or teleport using a whoopee cushion?

176. Would you rather wear clown shoes forever or a pirate hat that never comes off?

177. Would you rather have a never-ending bubble machine follow you or a parade of ducks?

178. Would you rather bounce instead of walk or spin in circles every time you sit down?

179. Would you rather sneeze glitter or fart bubbles?

180. Would you rather have spaghetti arms or crunchy cereal toes?

Monster Madness

Spooky, silly, and just the right amount of creepy - perfect for fearless gigglers.

181. Would you rather dance with a ghost or have lunch with a werewolf?

182. Would you rather have a pet zombie or a best friend who's a vampire?

183. Would you rather burp like a dragon or sneeze like a banshee?

184. Would you rather live in a haunted treehouse or a cave full of giggling goblins?

185. Would you rather have liquorice hair like Medusa or smell like a swamp monster?

186. Would you rather be chased by a giant slime monster or a pack of howling were-hamsters?

187. Would you rather be a mummy with toilet paper wrap or a robot powered by disco music?

188. Would you rather only be able to speak in spooky howls or creepy whispers?

189. Would you rather sleep on a bed of worms or share your bed with a giant eyeball?

190. Would you rather have monster feet or slime-dripping ears?

191. Would you rather sneeze spiders or hiccup bats?

192. Would you rather have glowing red eyes or fangs that chatter when you're scared?

193. Would you rather have a ghost as a teacher or a troll as a principal?

194. Would you rather be covered in fur like Bigfoot or scales like a sea monster?

195. Would you rather burp tiny lightning bolts or leave glow-in-the-dark footprints?

196. Would you rather your reflection turn into a monster or always follow you around?

197. Would you rather eat monster boogers or drink witch's stew?

198. Would you rather wear a costume made of bones or rotten candy?

199. Would you rather howl at the moon every night or snore like a zombie?

200. Would you rather get stuck in a vampire's library or a slime monster's playroom?

Fantasy Funnies

Magic, mayhem, and mythical mischief - your fairy tale just got totally bonkers.

201. Would you rather ride a unicorn that sneezes bubbles or fly a dragon that hiccups lightning?

202. Would you rather be best friends with a talking gnome or a sleepy giant?

203. Would you rather be a wizard without control or a fairy with stinky wings?

204. Would you rather have a wand that makes silly-string explosions or a cloak that smells like mouldy cheese?

205. Would you rather sleep in a cotton-candy or a cloud that smells like socks?

206. Would you rather grow a beard made of cotton candy or hair made of rainbows?

207. Would you rather sneeze out gold coins or fart stardust fog?

208. Would you rather turn into a frog every time you laugh or a dragon every time you cry?

209. Would you rather only eat enchanted mushrooms or magical slime?

210. Would you rather be a mermaid who can't swim or a centaur afraid of mud?

211. Would you rather slide down a rainbow or jump on clouds like trampolines?

212. Would you rather your best friend be a miniature ogre or a baby griffin?

213. Would you rather ride a magical potato or fly in a banana blimp?

214. Would you rather sneeze pixie dust or hiccup magic spells?

215. Would you rather battle a ticklish troll or a sneezy goblin?

216. Would you rather live in a shoe with elves or a pumpkin with a talking cat?

217. Would you rather be invisible but smell like garlic or glow in the dark but squeak when you walk?

218. Would you rather live in a candy-corn forest or a whipped-cream volcano?

219. Would you rather be a wizard with a spaghetti wand or a knight who rides a flying sausage?

220. Would you rather drink fizzy fairy soda or crunchy dragon snacks?

221. Would you rather have to sing everything you say in class or dance every time you enter a room?

222. Would you rather have a backpack that meows or notebooks that moo?

223. Would you rather take a math test underwater or do science experiments in outer space?

224. Would you rather have to hop to every class or crawl like a crab?

225. Would you rather sit on a jelly chair or write with a liquorice pen?

226. Would you rather have a locker that tells jokes or a desk that snores?

227. Would you rather have pencils that wiggle or erasers that explode into glitter?

228. Would you rather wear your gym uniform to every class or your pyjamas to the gym?

229. Would you rather have your teacher be a talking pineapple or a singing robot?

230. Would you rather your backpack be filled with whipped cream or mashed potatoes?

231. Would you rather the bell sound like a burp or a duck quack?

232. Would you rather take a spelling test where all the words are food or a history test where the answers are in riddles?

233. Would you rather eat lunch on a roller coaster or in the dark?

234. Would you rather get a gold star that talks or a sticker that won't stop dancing?

235. Would you rather be followed by a cloud that rains sprinkles or one that sneezes confetti?

236. Would you rather switch classes by zipline or sliding down a giant twisty slide?

237. Would you rather have to write essays in ketchup or take notes with a feather dipped in slime?

238. Would you rather have a cafeteria that only serves dessert or one that only serves mystery meat?

239. Would you rather have gym class in a pool of jelly or on a trampoline floor?

240. Would you rather every class be taught by a hamster or by a sock puppet?

241. Would you rather fly on a broomstick or teleport by sneezing?

Ridiculous Routines

From sunrise to bedtime, these daily doings are anything but ordinary.

242. Would you rather brush your teeth with syrup or shower in whipped cream?

243. Would you rather get dressed by a tornado or have to put on clothes with tongs?

244. Would you rather wake up every morning to a trumpet solo or a chicken dance parade?

245. Would you rather sleepwalk into a pudding pool or dream you're a walking spaghetti?

246. Would you rather your toothbrush sings opera or your soap farts bubbles?

247. Would you rather eat breakfast while bouncing on a trampoline or hanging upside down?

248. Would you rather have shoes that honk or pants that giggle?

249. Would you rather comb your hair with a spaghetti fork or brush it with a porcupine?

250. Would you rather your alarm clock be a yelling goat or a kazoo-playing duck?

251. Would you rather slide to school on a banana peel or hop there on one foot?

252. Would you rather your lunch was packed by a robot that only knows weird food or a raccoon in a chef hat?

253. Would you rather walk your dog while riding a unicycle or bike with a penguin?

254. Would you rather eat pancakes with chopsticks or cereal with a ladle?

255. Would you rather brush your teeth with whipped cream or shampoo with slime?

256. Would you rather have to hop every time you take a step or spin in a circle before opening a door?

257. Would you rather always lose your socks or wear them on your hands?

258. Would you rather eat dinner with your feet or sleep standing up like a flamingo?

259. Would you rather wear your clothes backwards for a month or only wear Halloween costumes to school?

260. Would you rather have a bedtime story read by a walrus or a lullaby sung by a robot?

261. Would you rather brush your hair with cotton candy or tie it with spaghetti?

Planet of the Pranks

Guaranteed giggles and harmless hijinks - prank responsibly!

262. Would you rather prank your teacher with a whoopee cushion or fill their desk with balloons?

263. Would you rather your shoes squeak super loudly or make fart noises with every step?

264. Would you rather swap your friend's sandwich with a rubber one or their drink with jelly?

265. Would you rather be invisible when someone says "banana" or turn bright purple when you giggle?

266. Would you rather cover everything you touch in glitter or spaghetti sauce?

267. Would you rather have prank gum that sprays juice or exploding candy?

268. Would you rather only be able to speak in rhymes or only talk using sock puppets?

269. Would you rather have a whoopee cushion you can't turn off or a fart horn for a voice?

270. Would you rather prank call aliens or send stink bombs to space pirates?

271. Would you rather switch places with a mime for a day or a clown in a tutu?

272. Would you rather live in a house made of bubble wrap or a room filled with ping-pong balls?

273. Would you rather always carry a water balloon or a banana peel?

274. Would you rather sneeze glitter or hiccup confetti?

275. Would you rather prank your whole class with rubber chickens or exploding cupcakes?

276. Would you rather have hands that shoot silly string or feet that leave jelly footprints?

277. Would you rather every joke you tell be a song or every laugh come out as a honk?

278. Would you rather wear a gorilla suit to a wedding or dress as a pickle at the zoo?

279. Would you rather have to say "Gotcha!" after every sentence or yell "Banana pants!" whenever you're surprised?

280. Would you rather be followed by a tuba player or a squeaky duck?

281. Would you rather fill your bathtub with pudding or prank your sibling with slime daily?

Bizarre Body Mix-Ups

Swap it, stretch it, or sparkle it - your body will never be the same again.

282. Would you rather have rubber-band arms or marshmallow legs?

283. Would you rather have jelly for bones or rubber for skin?

284. Would you rather sneeze spaghetti or cry ketchup?

285. Would you rather have broccoli growing out of your ears or carrots for your fingers?

286. Would you rather hiccup bubbles or burp confetti?

287. Would you rather have a nose that honks like a clown horn or ears that flap when you talk?

288. Would you rather have wheels instead of feet or springs for legs?

289. Would you rather have hair that sings or teeth that glow in the dark?

290. Would you rather have eyes on your knees or a tongue that tells jokes?

291. Would you rather have fingers that turn into crayons or feet that smell like egg sandwiches?

292. Would you rather have a rainbow-coloured tongue or glittery fingernails that never stop sparkling?

293. Would you rather grow a new toe every week or shed your eyebrows daily?

294. Would you rather have a moustache made of worms or eyelashes made of spaghetti?

295. Would you rather have one giant foot or three tiny feet?

296. Would you rather have a belly button that sings or knees that giggle?

297. Would you rather have a tail that wags when you lie or cheeks that light up when you're embarrassed?

298. Would you rather have elbows that squeak or a neck that stretches like a giraffe?

299. Would you rather have a hand that acts like a puppet or a foot that tries to dance on its own?

300. Would you rather grow feathers when cold or scales when embarrassed?

301. Would you rather swap your nose with your ear or your toes with your fingers?

Wacky Weather Wonders

Forecast: 100% chance of weird -from spaghetti rain to glitter storms.

302. Would you rather have it rain marshmallows or snow mashed potatoes?

303. Would you rather have a personal storm cloud that follows you or a sunbeam that makes you dance?

304. Would you rather ride a tornado like a rollercoaster or slide down a rainbow?

305. Would you rather get blown away by a sneezing wind or rained on by pickle juice?

306. Would you rather live where it's always foggy with glitter or where it rains jelly beans every afternoon?

307. Would you rather wear a raincoat made of marshmallows or boots filled with pudding?

308. Would you rather fly a kite in a cotton candy storm or splash in lemonade puddles?

309. Would you rather be stuck on a windy day that messes your hair or a foggy one where you can't stop sneezing?

310. Would you rather be the weather forecaster who only predicts banana storms or blueberry hail?

311. Would you rather get stuck inside during a whipped cream blizzard or an earthquake of giggles?

Tech Trouble Time

Gadgets gone goofy - when technology gets totally bonkers.

312. Would you rather have a phone that only plays chicken sounds or a tablet that sneezes when you touch it?

313. Would you rather have a laptop that burps every time you type or a printer that sings off-key songs?

314. Would you rather be stuck in a video game where everything is covered in slime or one where everything is made of socks?

315. Would you rather have a virtual pet that won't stop dancing or a smartwatch that randomly squirts mustard?

316. Would you rather your keyboard be made of jelly or your mouse be a real live hamster?

317. Would you rather charge your devices by doing jumping jacks or by eating stinky cheese?

318. Would you rather have glasses that show everything upside down or headphones that make everything sound like farts?

319. Would you rather play a video game using only your nose or scroll your phone with your tongue?

320. Would you rather have an alarm clock that yells jokes or a TV that won't stop tickling you when you watch it?

Sneaky Switch-Ups

Life's more fun when everything's in the wrong
place - let the mix-ups begin!

321. Would you rather swap noses with a pig or ears with
an elephant?

322. Would you rather trade voices with a parrot or laugh
like a donkey forever?

323. Would you rather switch your arms for spaghetti or
your legs for pogo sticks?

324. Would you rather have jellyfish tentacles instead of
fingers or octopus suckers on your toes?

325. Would you rather wear your clothes backwards forever or shoes on your hands?

326. Would you rather switch places with your pet for a day or with your teacher for a week?

327. Would you rather accidentally switch bodies with your sibling or your gym teacher?

328. Would you rather trade your hair with a mop or your teeth with candy corn?

329. Would you rather have to speak only in animal sounds or walk like a robot everywhere you go?

330. Would you rather have your hands swapped with your feet or your eyes swapped with your belly button?

331. Would you rather trade places with your lunchbox or your backpack for a day?

332. Would you rather your voice sound like a kazoo or a squeaky toy?

333. Would you rather have eyebrows that wiggle nonstop or knees that honk when you bend them?

334. Would you rather switch your arms for pool noodles or your feet for skateboards?

335. Would you rather sneeze feathers or hiccup bubbles every time you lie?

336. Would you rather switch your brain with a banana or your belly button with a whistle?

337. Would you rather be stuck in your friend's body or have your friend stuck in yours?

338. Would you rather switch your nose with a horn or your tongue with a sponge?

339. Would you rather have your laugh swapped with a goat's bleat or your sneeze with a trumpet sound?

340. Would you rather swap your reflection with a cartoon or your shadow with a jelly monster?

Outrageous Outdoors

Fresh air, wild adventures, and a sprinkle of total silliness.

341. Would you rather camp in a haunted tent or sleep in a tree full of squirrels?

342. Would you rather have bug spray that smells like cheese or sunscreen that's purple and sparkly?

343. Would you rather hike up a mountain made of jelly or swim through a lake of chocolate pudding?

344. Would you rather race a snail or have a staring contest with a frog?

345. Would you rather ride a unicycle through mud or slide down a grassy hill wearing banana peels?

346. Would you rather get chased by a swarm of giggling bees or be followed by a duck that tells bad jokes?

347. Would you rather climb a tree covered in spaghetti or jump rope with vines that giggle?

348. Would you rather go fishing and catch a singing fish or a dancing worm?

349. Would you rather explore a cave made of candy or a forest full of burping trees?

350. Would you rather have to tiptoe across a field of jelly mud or hop through a meadow of whipped cream?

351. Would you rather go cloud diving into mashed potatoes or ride a rainbow-powered zipline?

352. Would you rather eat giant marshmallows toasted by dragon fire or corn on the cob cooked by lightning?

353. Would you rather build a snowman that talks or a sandcastle that sings?

354. Would you rather be rained on by lemon soda or snowed on with mini marshmallows?

355. Would you rather jump in puddles that squeak or roll down a hill that giggles?

356. Would you rather catch a butterfly that tells jokes or a firefly that farts sparkles?

357. Would you rather mow the lawn using your teeth or rake leaves with your elbows

358. Would you rather ride a skateboard pulled by turtles or a scooter powered by burps?

359. Would you rather go canoeing in a gravy river or build a raft from pepperoni pizza?

360. Would you rather sleep in a hammock made of liquorice or a tent of toffee popcorn?

House of Havoc

Where home sweet home turns into home sweet chaos.

361. Would you rather have your bed replaced with a giant sponge or a trampoline?

362. Would you rather every door in your house make fart sounds or burp when you open it?

363. Would you rather have floors that are sticky syrup or covered in marbles?

364. Would you rather your fridge randomly yell "I'm hungry!" or shoot out whipped cream when opened?

365. Would you rather take a bubble bath in ketchup or brush your teeth with mustard?

366. Would you rather have a toilet that cheers when you sit or plays music when you flush?

367. Would you rather sleep in a bathtub full of jelly or a closet full of teddy bears?

368. Would you rather your lights flicker with disco music or your TV only play cartoons in reverse?

369. Would you rather your couch be made of jelly beans or your rug be a giant whoopee cushion?

370. Would you rather all your books be made of toast or all your toys be made of macaroni?

371. Would you rather slide down the stairs on a banana peel or bounce down on a giant marshmallow?

372. Would you rather have pillows that moo or blankets that bark?

373. Would you rather get tucked in by a robot or a singing llama?

374. Would you rather live in a house shaped like a doughnut or a dinosaur?

375. Would you rather have wallpaper that changes faces every day or floors that giggle when you walk?

376. Would you rather have to crawl everywhere in your house or hop like a kangaroo?

377. Would you rather the kitchen only cook food that squeaks or the bathroom only flush in slow motion?

378. Would you rather your laundry sing opera or your dishes tell jokes?

379. Would you rather have windows that open into candy land or stairs that turn into slides?

380. Would you rather your doorbell scream "TACO TIME!" or whisper secrets when pressed?

Bonkers Birthdays

Parties packed with pranks, cake chaos, and balloon buffoonery.

381. Would you rather have a birthday cake made of slime or one that explodes with glitter?

382. Would you rather unwrap presents that moo or ones that squirt whipped cream?

383. Would you rather your birthday party be run by penguins or dancing robots?

384. Would you rather wear a party hat that farts or shoes that honk with each step?

385. Would you rather blow out candles that shoot out jelly or burp confetti?

386. Would you rather be sung to by a goat choir or a kazoo band?

387. Would you rather open a gift that screams "SURPRISE!" or giggles nonstop?

388. Would you rather your balloons pop with spaghetti or launch into space when touched?

389. Would you rather have a cake made of pickles or cupcakes made of broccoli?

390. Would you rather play pin the tail on a hippo or musical chairs with monkeys?

Time Travel Trouble

Leap through history (and the future) with
maximum mayhem.

391. Would you rather visit the time of dinosaurs or a
future full of aliens?

392. Would you rather ride a time-travelling toilet or a
rocket-powered rocking chair?

393. Would you rather get stuck in the 1800s with a
smartphone or in the year 3000 with a horse?

394. Would you rather meet a caveman who only speaks
in burps or a robot that only raps?

395. Would you rather accidentally invent jelly beans or
the world's stickiest glue?

396. Would you rather swap places with your great-great-grandparent or your future grandkid?

397. Would you rather live in a world where dinosaurs do ballet or robots wear pyjamas?

398. Would you rather time travel every time you sneeze or hiccup?

399. Would you rather have a time machine shaped like a banana or a taco?

400. Would you rather get stuck in a medieval feast or a moon colony pizza party?

Pet Pandemonium

From jet-packing hamsters to skateboarding turtles - welcome to the wild side of pet ownership.

401. Would you rather have a cat that can juggle or a dog that can sing?

402. Would you rather walk a pet octopus or babysit a kangaroo?

403. Would you rather have a hamster with a jetpack or a turtle that rides a skateboard?

404. Would you rather your goldfish sing opera or your hamster write poems?

405. Would you rather share your room with a llama or a raccoon?

406. Would you rather have a pet goat that eats your homework or a snake that helps you with math?

407. Would you rather dress your pet in costumes every day or have them dress you?

408. Would you rather your pet bark your name or sing your favourite song?

409. Would you rather your pet grow to the size of an elephant or shrink to the size of a grape?

410. Would you rather have to groom a porcupine or bathe a skunk?

Sports Shenanigans

Game on! But get ready for the weirdest rules you've ever played by.

411. Would you rather play soccer with a beach ball or basketball with a watermelon?

412. Would you rather wear shoes full of pudding or gloves made of slime during a race?

413. Would you rather swim through Jelly or run across a peanut butter track?

414. Would you rather wrestle a marshmallow or race a giant turtle?

415. Would you rather only play sports with spaghetti or with invisible balls?

416. Would you rather have a cheering crowd of goats or squirrels?

417. Would you rather win a gold medal made of cheese or a trophy that sings?

418. Would you rather have a coach who only talks in riddles or one who burps instructions?

419. Would you rather play baseball with noodles or tennis with pies?

420. Would you rather play tag where everyone has jelly legs or hopscotch on whipped cream squares?

Costume Catastrophes

Dress-up disasters that are as funny as they are fashionable (or not).

421. Would you rather wear a hotdog costume every day or a dinosaur costume once a week?

422. Would you rather dress as a banana at weddings or as a pirate at the dentist's?

423. Would you rather wear a superhero cape that farts or clown shoes that giggle?

424. Would you rather only wear clothes made of paper or bubble wrap?

425. Would you rather dress as a robot at school or a unicorn at the grocery store?

426. Would you rather have a hat that plays music or pants that light up?

427. Would you rather have your costume come to life or chase you around the room?

428. Would you rather wear pyjamas to a fancy event or a tuxedo to gym class?

429. Would you rather dress like a taco for Halloween or a pickle for your birthday?

430. Would you rather your costume squeak when you walk or change colours when you talk?

Silly Sleepytime

Bedtime stories you won't believe - and definitely won't snooze through.

431. Would you rather snore glitter or sleepwalk while breakdancing?

432. Would you rather dream in cartoons or only dream in sound effects?

433. Would you rather wear a hat that snores or slippers that meow?

434. Would you rather your blanket randomly tickle you or your pillow yell jokes?

435. Would you rather sleep on a trampoline or on a bed of marshmallows?

436. Would you rather get tucked in by a walrus or a wizard?

437. Would you rather only sleep upside-down like a bat or while spinning like a top?

438. Would you rather your dreams be narrated by a llama or a pirate?

439. Would you rather sleepwalk into a bathtub of spaghetti or a room of giggling ghosts?

440. Would you rather have a bedtime story read by a robot or sung by a chicken?

Holiday Hijinks

Festive fun with a totally wacky twist.

441. Would you rather get a Halloween costume of cheese or Easter eggs full of slime?

442. Would you rather decorate your tree with socks or your house with underpants?

443. Would you rather have a turkey that sings or an elf that snores?

444. Would you rather celebrate your birthday every week or Halloween every day?

445. Would you rather find a present that farts or candy that dances?

446. Would you rather get Valentine's cards from skunks or chocolate from raccoons?

447. Would you rather wear bunny ears year-round or jingle bells on your shoes forever?

448. Would you rather open gifts that moo or ones that squirt bubbles?

449. Would you rather meet a snowman who burps or a reindeer who tells jokes?

450. Would you rather celebrate a holiday where everyone wears pyjamas or eats spaghetti for breakfast?

Giggle Games

Every game night needs a little chaos - and these deliver it in spades.

451. Would you rather play tag with invisible friends or hide and seek with a talking sandwich?

452. Would you rather jump into a pit of whipped cream or bounce on a jellybean trampoline?

453. Would you rather play dodgeball with pies or musical chairs where the chairs moo?

454. Would you rather your board game pieces be live worms or jelly cubes?

455. Would you rather play Twister on a floor made of bananas or hopscotch on spaghetti lines?

456. Would you rather win a trophy full of goo or a crown made of broccoli?

457. Would you rather your controller be covered in peanut butter or jelly?

458. Would you rather play charades with chickens or Pictionary with penguins?

459. Would you rather have a game night where you can only yell or only burp to communicate?

460. Would you rather play freeze tag and get stuck in a silly pose or one where you quack when tagged?

Alien Adventures

Out-of-this-world silliness that's truly spaced out.

461. Would you rather be abducted by aliens who juggle slime-covered doughnuts or ones who sing karaoke?

462. Would you rather eat lunch on a spaceship or dinner on Mars?

463. Would you rather your best friend be an alien with five eyes or one with tentacle arms?

464. Would you rather explore a planet made of bubblegum or socks?

465. Would you rather your alien spaceship smell like old cheese or sound like a whoopee cushion?

466. Would you rather speak only in alien beeps or be translated by a talking toilet?

467. Would you rather your space suit be made of bubble wrap or glow sticks?

468. Would you rather ride a meteor to school or a moon buggy shaped like a taco?

469. Would you rather live with aliens who burp to say hello or fart to say goodbye?

470. Would you rather have an alien dance battle or a slime wrestling match?

Silly Circus

Roll up, roll up! The funniest show on Earth is about to begin.

471. Would you rather be a clown who only tells knock-knock jokes or one who sneezes glitter?

472. Would you rather juggle pies or ride a unicycle on pudding?

473. Would you rather have cotton candy hair or popcorn shoes?

474. Would you rather do tricks with a sneezing elephant or a hiccupping lion?

475. Would you rather perform a dance with dancing monkeys or singing turtles?

476. Would you rather be shot out of a cannon full of feathers or bubbles?

477. Would you rather eat spaghetti from a top hat or popcorn from a clown shoe?

478. Would you rather train a bear to disco dance or a flamingo to rap?

479. Would you rather have circus music follow you everywhere or walk on stilts for a week?

480. Would you rather sleep in a clown car or on a trampoline tent?

Magical Mayhem

Spells, potions, and magical mishaps - expect the unexpected.

481. Would you rather pull rabbits from your ears or frogs from your shoes?

482. Would you rather cast a spell that makes things fly or one that makes them burp?

483. Would you rather have a wand that sneezes glitter or onc that farts bubbles?

484. Would you rather ride a broomstick that tells jokes or one that sings opera?

485. Would you rather be turned into a lollipop or a chocolate bar for a day?

486. Would you rather have a potion that makes you super bouncy or super stinky?

487. Would you rather have a pet dragon that snores lightning or one that hiccups fire?

488. Would you rather go to wizard school in a volcano or an ice cream castle?

489. Would you rather have your magic spell backfire and turn you into a chicken or a frog?

490. Would you rather your wand be made of noodles or rubber chickens?

Totally Random Ridiculousness

No theme, no rules - just pure, unfiltered silliness.

491. Would you rather have spaghetti hair or syrup toes?

492. Would you rather sneeze pickles or fart bubbles?

493. Would you rather live in a giant shoe or a humongous hat?

494. Would you rather have your hands replaced with bananas or your feet replaced with marshmallows?

495. Would you rather hiccup glitter or burp foghorn sounds?

496. Would you rather eat cereal with ketchup or pizza with jelly beans?

497. Would you rather only be able to whisper like a ghost or shout like a pirate?

498. Would you rather be followed by a polka-dotted duck or a rapping snail?

499. Would you rather have teeth that glow in the dark or ears that wiggle when you're happy?

Final Funny Frenzy

The ultimate round of bonkers fun - end on the biggest laugh.

500. Would you rather your nose honk like a horn when you sneeze or squeak like a rubber duck when you laugh?

501. Would you rather have jelly for muscles or whipped cream for bones?

502. Would you rather walk on stilts made of candy canes or bounce on shoes made of jelly?

503. Would you rather have eyebrows that do cartwheels or hair that sings lullabies?

504. Would you rather have a belly button that shoots confetti or tells jokes?

505. Would you rather have your burps smell like rotten eggs or your feet smell like cheese popcorn?

506. Would you rather have to dance every time someone says your name or make a chicken noise every time someone says "hello"?

507. Would you rather grow bananas from your fingers or sprout pancakes from your knees?

508. Would you rather have eyelashes made of noodles or fingernails made of gummy worms?

509. Would you rather wear a hat made of pickles or pants made of waffles?

510. Would you rather have a voice that only sings opera or sounds like a robot frog?

511. Would you rather ride a unicorn that burps starlight or a llama that sneezes rainbows?

512. Would you rather eat ice cream with mustard or cookies dipped in pickle juice?

513. Would you rather have a backpack full of slime or pockets filled with mashed potatoes?

514. Would you rather your laugh sound like a kazoo or a squeaky door?

515. Would you rather slide everywhere like on a banana peel or bounce like a pogo stick?

516. Would you rather be followed by a cloud that rains soda or one that drops cupcakes?

517. Would you rather brush your teeth with ketchup or wash your hair with syrup?

518. Would you rather hiccup tiny frogs or sneeze floating popcorn?

519. Would you rather always smell like french fries or sound like a squeaky toy when you walk?

Make Your Own Would You Rather?

Create your own wild, weird, and wacky questions
— your imagination's the limit.

Use the word banks to fill in the blanks and create your own gross, silly, and totally bonkers questions!

Would you rather eat a _ _ _ _ _ _ _ _ made of _ _ _ _ _ _ _ _ or wear a _ _ _ _ _ _ _ _ on your head for a week?

Would you rather burp _ _ _ _ _ _ _ _ every time you talk or sneeze out _ _ _ _ _ _ _ _ once a day?

Would you rather ride a _ _ _ _ _ _ _ _ to school or be followed everywhere by a _ _ _ _ _ _ _ _?

Would you rather sleep in a bed full of _ _ _ _ _ _ _ _ or brush your teeth with _ _ _ _ _ _ _ _?

Gross Stuff: pickle juice, toe jam, mouldy bananas, spaghetti and dirt, a sock full of slime

Silly Things: glitter, rainbow noodles, squeaky toys, whipped cream, upside-down pants

Weird Creatures & Animals: farting unicorn, chicken in sunglasses, disco llama, dancing robot, sneezy sloth

Totally Random Objects: sandwich hat, toilet plunger, talking backpack, jellybean shoes, slime cannon

Totally Bonkers Bingo

The only bingo game where weird, wacky, and
wonderful are the winning moves

**Mark an X on the things you've done or would totally
do. Can you get five in a row?**

Sniffed something weird

Made up your own animal

Laughed so hard you snorted

Wore socks on your hands

Pretended to be a robot

Danced in the rain

Ate something really gross

Said 'meow' in class

Made a weird face in the mirror

Tried to lick your elbow

Pretended the floor was lava

Wiggled like a worm

Talked in a silly voice

Tried not to laugh and failed

Wrote your own joke

Tried to walk backward all day

Sang in the shower

Put food on your head

Said 'Would you rather?' 10 times

Played a prank

Wore your shirt backwards

Built a blanket fort

Made a silly sound

Acted like a chicken

Farted and blamed someone else

Bonkers Drawing Challenge

Turn your silliest ideas into masterpieces that belong in the Museum of Totally Ridiculous Art.

Grab a pencil and get ready to draw your way into total silliness! Try these:

1. Draw what it would look like if your hair was made of spaghetti.

2. Draw yourself riding a dinosaur through a grocery store.

3. Draw what it would look like if your best friend turned into a fart cloud.

4. Draw the grossest snack you can imagine.

5. Draw a super silly creature that's part llama, part pizza

6. Draw a toilet that can fly and takes you to school.

7. Draw yourself as a superhero whose only power is making fart noises.

8. Draw a sandwich with eyeballs, tentacles, and roller skates

9. Draw what you'd look like if you swapped heads with your pet

Gross-Out Hall of Fame

You've seen some seriously gross questions... but which ones deserve an award?

Nominate your top picks below:

The one that made me gag the most:

The one I'd actually try (but don't tell anyone):

The weirdest answer I gave:

Winner of the Golden Booger Award:

Totally True, Totally Bonkers Facts!

Real facts that sound made up – but aren't!

Animal Oddities

- A snail can sleep for up to three years without eating. Talk about lazy!

- There are more plastic flamingos on Earth than real ones. The lawn kind wins.

- Wombats make cube-shaped poo so it doesn't roll away. Handy, huh?

- Cows have best friends and get upset when they're apart. Moo-mates forever!

- Sharks are older than trees - they've been swimming for over 400 million years.

- An octopus has three hearts and blue blood. One for love, two for extra drama.

- Some frogs freeze solid in winter and thaw back to life in spring. Nature's popsicles!

- Koalas have fingerprints so similar to ours they can confuse detectives.

- A sloth can hold its breath longer than a dolphin - up to 40 minutes!

Humans Are Weird Too

- If you stretched out all your blood vessels, they'd wrap around the Earth twice.

- Your stomach grows a new lining every few days so it doesn't digest itself.

- Your feet make about a cup of sweat each day. Gross but true!

- Sneezes can travel up to 100 miles per hour. Gesundheit and duck!

- Your belly button is home to thousands of tiny bacteria – some found nowhere else on Earth.

- Humans share about 60% of their DNA with bananas. Maybe that explains why we slip on them.

- Elephants are the only mammals that can't jump - and humans can't wiggle their ears like them, so call it even.

Weird Wonders of Science

- There's a jellyfish that can live forever by "resetting" itself – the immortal blob!

- Ants don't have lungs - they breathe through holes along their bodies.

- Some lizards squirt blood from their eyes to scare predators. Ew, but genius.

- A shrimp's heart is in its head. That's one way to stay level-headed.

- The fingerprints of lemurs are almost identical to humans'. Even science struggles to tell us apart.

- Butterflies can taste with their feet. Snack time just got strange!

Bizarre World Wonders

- There's a lake in Africa called Lake Natron that's so salty it can turn animals into statues! (They look frozen but it's just minerals.)

- In Yoro, Honduras, it sometimes rains fish after heavy storms!

- Iceland has no mosquitoes. Not one. They just don't like it there.

- Australia once went to war with emus... and lost! (The birds were too fast.)

- Jellyfish have lived on Earth for over 500 million years – they're older than dinosaurs!

- In Antarctica, scientists found a waterfall that's bright red – it's called Blood Falls (but it's really rusty salt water).

- There's a town in Norway where the sun doesn't rise for two whole months each winter. (Bedtime forever!)

- In Japan, you can find square watermelons – they grow them in boxes to fit in fridges better.

- A volcano in Indonesia sometimes spews blue lava because it burns sulphur gas.

- Lightning can strike the same place twice - there's a lake in Venezuela that gets hit thousands of times a night!

The Bonkers Fact Challenge!

Ready for the ultimate test of your gross, silly, and totally bonkers brainpower? Try this quiz of real-but-ridiculous facts and see how many you can guess! No peeking at the answers — they're hiding on the next page. Grab a pencil, a brave friend, and prepare to be amazed (or mildly horrified).

1. What animal has green bones that glow under UV light?

2. What vegetable was once used as money in ancient Egypt?

3. How many noses does a slug have?

4. Which animal's milk is bright pink?

5. What body part never stops growing your whole life?

6. Which fruit used to be called a "love apple"?

7. What creature can regrow its own head after it's chopped off?

8. How many hearts does an earthworm have?

9. Which animal's teeth never stop growing?

10. What food was invented by accident when a kid left his drink outside overnight?

11. Which bird can sleep while flying?

12. What part of your body has no blood supply and heals itself very slowly?

13. Which animal has blue blood because of copper instead of iron?

14. What was the first animal sent into space?

15. Which bug farts the loudest compared to its size?

16. How many stomachs does a cow have?

17. What's the only part of your body that can't heal itself?

18. Which animal can turn its stomach inside out to clean it?

19. What happens if you cut a starfish in half?

20. What everyday food used to be so valuable it was traded for gold?

Bonkers Fact Challenge - Answers!

1. The green bone creature is a frog — the South American glass frog has glowing green bones!

2. Onions were used as currency in ancient Egypt (they even paid workers with them).

3. A slug has four noses — two for smelling and two for feeling.

4. Hippos have bright pink milk because of special acids in their sweat!

5. Your nose and ears never stop growing.

6. Tomatoes were once called "love apples" in Europe.

7. A type of flatworm can regrow its entire head — brain and all!

8. An earthworm has five hearts.

9. Rats and rabbits — their teeth grow nonstop, which is why they nibble everything.

10. Popsicles! They were invented when an 11-year-old left his soda outside one cold night.

11. The frigatebird can nap while flying long distances.

12. Your cornea (the clear part of your eye) has no blood supply and heals slowly.

13. Octopuses — their blood is blue because it's copper

14. Laika the dog was the first living creature in space.

15. The beetle — specifically the bombardier beetle — farts with explosive bursts!

16. A cow has four stomachs.

17. Your tooth enamel — once it's gone, it can't regrow.

18. Starfish and sea cucumbers can turn their stomachs inside out for cleaning or defence.

19. A starfish can grow into two new ones if both halves have part of the centre!

20. Salt was once traded ounce-for-ounce with gold.

Thank You and Bonus Features!

Thanks for reading! If this book made you giggle, gasp, or groan (in the best possible way), I'd love it if you left a short review. Your feedback helps other readers discover the fun and keeps the silliness going!

Enjoyed the book? Leave your review here, or use the QR code at the end of this section:

https://mybook.to/WYRGrossSillyBonkers

Get Even More Bonkers Fun!

As a special thank you, you can grab my Bonkers Bonus Pack – packed with:

- A Certificate of Bonkers Bravery

- Extra silly games like Spin-a-Dare and Debate Club

- Fill-in-the-blank challenges

- The Bonkers Joke Generator

- Colouring pages...and more!

Get it here: https://tinyurl.com/WYRBonusContent

Psst... Want More Laughs?

Check out my other books:

Brilliant Blunders & Fortunate Flops: 101 Random Facts, Funny Mistakes, and Stories of Inventions That Changed the World by Accident - perfect for curious kids who love hilarious surprises and real history that sounds made-up.

Inside you'll discover:

- How a bored chef's tantrum created the world's first crispy potato chip

- How a messy lab accident led to life-saving penicillin

- How a scientist trying to invent a super-strong glue accidentally created a very weak adhesive... which later became perfect for Post-it Notes

- How a failed heart experiment gave us the pacemaker that saves lives today

- How a kitchen accident turned into one of the world's most popular breakfast cereals

Packed with fun facts, laugh-out-loud twists, and surprising discoveries, this adventure will make you see every "oops" in a whole new way.

Available now on Amazon - see the QR code at the end of this section.

Love colouring?

Meet Funny Animals With Attitude!

A bold-outline colouring adventure full of silly animal characters, short stories, and fun facts.

Perfect for kids, teens, and adults who love creativity, relaxation, and giggles.

Psst!

The QR codes for your bonus pack and other fun extras are waiting at the end of this section – ready to jump out and surprise you!

Would You Rather Review

Would You Rather Bonus Content

Brilliant Blunders & Fortunate Flops

Funny Animals with Attitude Colouring Book

Certificate of Bonkers Bravery

This certifies that

_____

has completed every gross, silly, and totally bonkers
challenge in this book!

You are now officially a:

Gross-Out Guru · Silly Superstar · Bonkers Boss

Awarded by T. J. Harvey

About the Author

T J Harvey loves nothing more than making kids laugh until juice comes out their noses. She's a part-time gummy worm gobbler, full-time inventor of the weirdest, wackiest, and most wonderfully ridiculous "Would You Rather?" questions on the planet.

Whether it's a stinky sock debate or a choice between burping rainbows and sneezing glitter, she's probably written it - and giggled the whole time.

When she's not busy dreaming up bonkers Would You Rather scenarios for Max and Princess Ruby, you might spot her riding an invisible unicorn through the grocery store, talking to squirrels, or holding a serious meeting with her pet rock collection.

T J believes that being silly is serious business – and the best kind of fun. She hopes her books bring belly laughs, loud snorts, and a whole lot of imagination to kids everywhere.

Afterword

Don't forget to keep the silly going and be totally bonkers whenever you can - just do it safely... so probably best not to include a dragon!

TJ

Printed in Dunstable, United Kingdom

73525265R00067